DANIEL BOONE

KATHARINE ELLIOTT WILKIE

ZINC READ

Published by
This edition copyright © 2024 by Zinc Read
Design and setting By Zinc Read
Email- zincread@gmail.com
ISBN-978-93-6748-697-9

CONTENTS

DANIEL'S INDIAN FRIEND

Daniel Boone was a boy who lived on the edge of the deep woods in Pennsylvania. At that time this country still belonged to England.

Friendly Indians often came out of the woods to visit the white men. Daniel liked the Indians. He liked them so well that he wished he could live with them.

One day he was taking care of his father's cattle. The pasture was several miles from the settlement. Although Daniel was a ten-year-old boy, he sometimes became lonely by himself.

Today he lay on a hillside and sang aloud. He wanted to hear a voice, even if it was only his own.

There was a low laugh behind him. Daniel sprang to his feet. A tall, slim Indian boy stood a few feet away. The white boy liked him at once.

"I sing, too," the young Indian said.

He threw back his head and sang. Daniel could not understand a word.

"I sing to the sun and the wind and the rain," the boy explained.

"I like your Indian song," Daniel said, "but I'm glad you speak English."

The boy patted the bow that hung over his right shoulder. "You like this?"

The bow was strong and shining. Daniel ran a finger along the smooth wood.

"I like it very much," he said.

The other boy took an arrow and placed it on the bowstring. He pulled back the bow. The arrow flew away.

"You get," the Indian said.

Daniel ran after the arrow. He picked it up and looked back. The Indian boy was right beside him.

He took the arrow from Daniel. Again he shot it. Again the white boy ran after it. The young Indian ran beside him.

He shook his head when Daniel handed him the arrow.

He handed Daniel the bow.

"Shoot!" he said.

Daniel took the bow in his hands. He pulled it back and let the arrow fly.

By now Daniel had forgotten the cattle. He had forgotten everything but the wonderful bow, his new friend, and the wide, wild woods.

After a while the boys came to a high hill. At the bottom was an Indian village. The brown-skinned boy took Daniel by the hand and ran toward the settlement.

Several dogs barked at them. Some women were hoeing their gardens. They hardly looked up as the boys passed.

An old woman was stirring something in an iron pot over a fire. It smelled good. Daniel remembered that he had eaten nothing since breakfast.

His friend stopped and pointed to Daniel and himself. The old woman nodded. With a sharp stick, she lifted a piece of meat from the pot.

The Indian boy took a broad leaf from a near-by bush. The woman dropped the hot meat on it.

Now Daniel knew what to do. He, too, found a leaf. The woman gave him some meat. Soon the hungry boys had finished their lunch.

That afternoon they swam in the clear, broad river. Then they lay on the bank in the sunshine. Daniel had never been so happy. However, he knew he must soon go home. His mother would worry if he did not return before dark.

"I must go now. I must drive the cows home," he told his Indian friend.

The boy frowned. "Women's work," he told Daniel.

Daniel laughed. "It may be for the Indians, but it's not at the Boones' house. I think I'd like being an Indian. An Indian boy has more fun than a white boy."

"There is much for an Indian to learn," the other told him. "We must learn to hunt, track animals, fish, and find our way in the wilderness."

"Those things are not work. They are fun," Daniel told him. "I wish I were an Indian. I believe I'd make a better Indian than a white boy."

When Daniel reached home at last, his mother scolded him.

"You should not have gone off with that Indian boy. You can't trust the Indians," she told her son.

"He was a good boy. I liked him," Daniel said.

His mother shook her head. "Indians are not like us. We think differently from them."

Daniel said nothing. But he thought his mother was mistaken.

"*I believe I can think like an Indian,*" he said to himself. "*Except for color, I'm more like an Indian than a white boy.*"

MOVING ON

Several years went by. Then Father Boone called the family together. "Pack your things," he told them. "We are leaving here. Boones never stay long in one place. Besides, our farm land is worn out. We can buy rich land cheap to the southwest of here. We will settle there."

Sixteen-year-old Daniel was happy. "I'm glad we are going," he said. "I feel crowded here. There are too many houses and too many people. And the game is getting scarce."

Father Boone made ready for the journey. He got out the big wagon and hitched two horses to it. Mother Boone packed clothes, quilts, dishes, pots, pans, and kettles. She would fix food for the family along the way. Daniel tied a cow behind the wagon.

The family said good-by to the neighbors and to their old home, and started. Mother, the girls, and the little children rode in the wagon. Father and the boys took turns riding the horses. Sometimes all of the Boones walked so that the horses could rest. Father and the boys had guns to kill birds and small animals for food along the way.

The Boones traveled across Pennsylvania. On and on they went toward the new country. Daniel caught many rabbits, which his mother stewed. Once he shot a small black bear. Another time he killed a deer. This gave the Boones food for several days.

At last the family came to the rolling, green Yadkin Valley in North Carolina. There were a few houses there already, but it was much wilder than in Pennsylvania.

Father Boone said, "This is good farming land. We will stop here."

Daniel looked all about him. There was level land close by. There were woods not far away. And there were mountains in the west. Daniel knew the hunting would be good.

"I like this place," he said. "There's plenty of room here."

Father Boone and the boys jumped off the horses. Mother Boone and the girls climbed down from the wagon. They fed the horses and the cow. They made a campfire. Father and the boys cut down trees and started to build a log house. Soon the Boones had a new home in the new land.

The years went by. Daniel grew taller. His shoulders became wider. He was fair-haired and blue-eyed, lean and rugged. He hunted in the woods of the Yadkin Valley. He often brought home deer and bear. The Boones' neighbors said that Daniel was the best shot for miles around. Daniel Boone had grown up.

A KNOCK AT THE DOOR

When Daniel Boone was a young man, there was war between England and France. England sent troops to fight against the French in America. The French claimed the land west of the mountains. The English claimed the same land. The Indians sided with the French.

Daniel Boone drove a supply wagon for the English and the Americans. He made friends with another young wagoner named John Finley. Finley had been to the land southwest of the mountains. Each night he and Boone sat by the campfire and talked.

"I've been deep in the wilderness they call Kentucky," Finley told Boone. "It is a wonderful place. The forests go on and on and on. There are thousands of buffalo in Kentucky. There are deer, bear and small animals, too. It is a great land for hunters."

"I want to go there," Daniel said.

"There are Indians in the wilderness," Finley told Daniel. "They live to the north of Kentucky and to the south of Kentucky. They call the land their hunting ground. They do not like the white men to go there."

"There should be room enough for both Indians and white men," Daniel Boone replied. He thought for a while. "Some day I am going to Kentucky."

When Daniel went back home to the Yadkin Valley, he married a tall, dark-haired girl named Rebecca Bryan. Sometimes he liked to tease her. One summer day before they married he was sitting beside her under a big tree. Suddenly he took his broad-bladed knife and cut a long slit in her fresh white apron.

"Why did you do that, Daniel?" she asked mildly.

His blue eyes twinkled. "I guess I wanted to see if you had a temper," he said.

Because she wasn't angry, Daniel felt that she would make him a good wife. Life in the wilderness was often difficult and dangerous. He wanted a wife who did not become upset easily.

They were married, and soon the first of their many children arrived. Daniel loved his children. As soon as his son James was old enough, he taught him to hunt.

In the spring and summer Daniel would farm. In the autumn he hunted, and in the winter he trapped. He made long trips in the forest and brought home food for his family and valuable furs and deerskins.

Many of these he sold. He enjoyed exploring as much as he enjoyed hunting. Once he even went as far south as Florida with the idea of settling there. But he was disappointed in the land. He longed to explore Kentucky, but did not want to go alone.

One day the Boone family heard a knock at the door. It was Boone's old friend, John Finley.

"Let's go to Kentucky, Daniel!" he said.

"Let's!" Daniel agreed. "I think about it all the time. You know how much I love the wilderness. That's the one place I really feel at home."

ON TO KENTUCKY

Early in 1769, Daniel Boone, John Finley, and four other strong men started for Kentucky. One of the men was Daniel's brother-in-law. They took their guns. They carried animal traps, too. They planned to bring back skins and furs to sell.

The hunters rode their horses across the mountains. Soon they came to Cumberland Gap, a narrow mountain valley which led into Kentucky. The Indians used the Gap also, but the white men did not see any of them at this time. It was weeks before they saw a single Indian.

But they did see rich green meadows, which stretched ahead for miles. Silver rivers wound like ribbons through them. In some places there were low rolling hills and in others great towering mountains. The woods were thick and still. The sunlight made dancing patterns on the pine needles. Kentucky was as beautiful as John Finley had said.

Everywhere they went the men found lots of game. There were deer and buffalo. There were fur-bearing animals, such as mink and otter and beaver. There were many different kinds of birds.

When the men went hunting, they separated into pairs. One winter day Boone and his brother-in-law were captured by Indians. The Indians did not harm them, but they took all the white men's deerskins.

"Get out of Kentucky and stay out!" the Indians told them.

Daniel Boone did not scare easily. He and his brother-in-law did not want to leave Kentucky.

But the other four were afraid. They returned to the settlements. Boone never saw Finley again. But Boone was soon joined by his brother, Squire, and a friend named Alexander Neeley. Squire had promised to harvest the crops back home and then join them in the late autumn with fresh horses, traps, and gunpowder. Skilled woodsmen that they were, the brothers somehow found each other in the wilderness.

While they were hunting, the men separated again. They met every two weeks. One week Boone's brother-in-law did not return to camp. He never did come back. Five years later a skeleton with a powder horn beside it was found in a hollow tree. Perhaps he was wounded by an Indian. No one really knows what happened to him.

Neeley was scared. He decided to go home alone. But Daniel and Squire stayed on all winter and spring. They hunted and trapped until they had a lot of skins. Then Squire went home to sell the skins and buy more gunpowder and traps.

Daniel stayed on in the wilderness. He did not mind being alone. He was never afraid. With his trusty rifle, Tick-Licker, over his shoulder, he explored much of Kentucky. He was happy because the wilderness was wide and he felt free. After a few months, Squire came back. Again the brothers hunted together.

At last Daniel said to Squire, "I'll go home with you this time. We have all the skins we can carry."

"When we sell them, we'll have plenty of money to take to our families," Squire said happily.

It did not happen that way. Indians attacked the brothers when they were nearly home and took the skins. The Boones were still poor men.

But Daniel was happy. He was glad that he had roamed the wilderness for nearly two years. He was sorry he had lost the skins, but he was happy that he had seen Kentucky.

ATTACKED BY INDIANS

Two years later Daniel Boone decided that he had been away from Kentucky long enough. "Pack up, Rebecca," he said to his wife. "Pack up, children. We Boones can't stay in one spot forever. We're going to move to Kentucky. It's wild and beautiful there. There'll be plenty of land for you young ones when you want homes of your own."

So the Boones packed up. Six other families joined them. People always seemed ready to join Daniel in his search for adventure. The household goods and the farm tools were piled on pack horses. A few of the people rode horseback. But most of them walked. They drove their pigs and cattle before them. The rough trails made travel slow, but the families did not seem to mind.

Just before they reached Cumberland Gap, Daniel Boone sent his sixteen-year-old son, James, on an errand.

"Turn back to Captain Russell's cabin and ask him for the farm tools he and I were talking about," he told the boy. "You can catch up with us tomorrow."

James reached Captain Russell's safely. He camped that night with several men who planned to join Boone. In the darkness some Indians crept up and killed them all.

When the families with Boone heard the news, they no longer wanted to go to Kentucky. They turned and went back over the mountains. The Boone family was sad because of James' death. But Daniel would not give up his dream of living in Kentucky. It would just have to wait a little. He took his wife and children to a spot where they would be safe. But they did not go all the way back to the Yadkin Valley.

Daniel learned that all through the Kentucky Wilderness the Indians were fighting the white men.

Too many white men were coming west. Indians wanted to keep their hunting grounds for themselves. Daniel Boone and another man went into Kentucky to warn the surveyors who were measuring land there. Nearly all of them escaped safely. For a time, the Indians stopped fighting and Kentucky was peaceful again.

THE WILDERNESS ROAD

Now a rich man named Richard Henderson had a big idea. He would try to buy Kentucky from the Indians for himself and start another colony. His own company would sell land to settlers. Henderson was Daniel's friend. Boone had talked to the Indians about the idea and thought they would sell the land. Many Indian tribes hunted in Kentucky, but the Cherokees were the most important. They had conquered the other tribes and ruled the land. Henderson sent Boone to ask the Cherokees to meet him at Sycamore Shoals in what is now Tennessee.

Twelve hundred Indian men, women, and children came to the meeting place. Henderson had all his trading goods spread out. There were yards and yards of red cloth. There were hundreds of bright new guns. There were beads and pins and little mirrors for the women. Henderson's company had paid a great deal of money for the trading goods.

The Indians were like children about the business of trading land for goods. They loved the bright-colored trinkets. But they knew nothing about the value of land.

Although they had their own lawyer, they traded Kentucky to Henderson for a tiny part of what it was worth. The Cherokees warned the white men of savage Indians who came hunting from the west and the north. They told Henderson he might have trouble settling the land.

Boone did not go with Henderson to Sycamore Shoals. He waited near Cumberland Gap with thirty men. When Henderson sent word that he had bought Kentucky, Boone spoke one word to his men.

"Start!" he said.

The men began to make the famous Wilderness Road that was to lead to Kentucky. Later it would be traveled by settlers with their horses, wagons, and cattle. Just now Boone's men chose the shortest and easiest way over the mountains and through the woods. They followed Indian trails and buffalo paths. They swung their axes. They cut down trees. They crossed streams. Daniel Boone worked as hard as anyone. And all the time he kept a sharp lookout for unfriendly Indians.

The men did not stop until they reached the banks of the Kentucky River. Here they began to build a fort. Boone knew that the Shawnees and other Indian tribes would not admit that Henderson had bought Kentucky.

When Henderson came to the settlement, he said, "We will call this place Boonesborough. It is right to name it for the man who led us here."

Boone went back to get his family. Some of his children had grown up and married before the Boones set out for Kentucky the first time. Thirteen-year-old Jemima was his last unmarried daughter. She and her mother were the first white women to stand on the bank of the Kentucky River.

THE RESCUE

One Sunday afternoon, Jemima and two other girls went for a canoe ride on the Kentucky River at Boonesborough. They knew they should not go out of sight of the fort, but they went anyway. They paddled down the river and around the bend. The current drew them in to the opposite bank.

"Let's land and pick some of those bright-colored flowers," one of the girls suggested.

Jemima shook her head. "I'm afraid of the Indians," she said. "Those Shawnees are mean."

By now the canoe had drifted near the shore. The girl at the bow shoved with her paddle. The boat would not move. It was stuck fast in the mud.

All at once five Indians leaped from the underbrush. They grabbed the screaming girls and carried them into the forest. They planned to take them north to the Indian towns and keep them there as slaves.

Back at the fort no one missed the girls until after dark. Then someone saw that the canoe was gone. When Daniel Boone heard this, he picked up his gun and rushed toward the river. He did not stop to put on his shoes.

He felt sure that Indians had taken Jemima and her friends away.

Three young men who loved the girls very much went with Boone. The men took another canoe and began to paddle down the river. They could not go far in the dark. Before long, they had to stop and wait for morning.

When the sun came up, Boone found the girls' trail. He thought the Indians were taking them toward the Ohio River. He knew he must catch them before they crossed it and went to the Indian towns in the north.

The white men left their canoe. They traveled all day through the deep woods. Then they made camp and waited for the long night to end. At daylight they started out again.

Boone took short cuts through the woods, but he always found the trail. His sharp eyes saw what the girls had left for him to see. One had dug her heels into the soft mud. Another had left bits of her dress here and there.

Boone led the young men straight through the heart of the forest to Jemima and her friends. About noon the men caught sight of the girls.

The Indians had stopped with them for their noon meal. The white men crept up. Bang! Bang! Bang! went their guns.

"It's Father!" Jemima cried.

"Fall flat on your faces, girls!" Daniel Boone shouted.

The white men ran toward the Indians. They shot their guns as they ran.

The Indians were taken by surprise. One Indian threw his tomahawk. It almost hit the girls. Two Indians were shot. The others ran away.

The men took the three girls back to Boonesborough. Later the three girls married the three young men.

THE FORT IS SAVED

Boone became known far and wide as the greatest man in the Kentucky Wilderness. One winter, about a year after he had saved the girls from the Indians, he went with some other men to a place where there were salt springs. These were called salt licks because the wild animals liked to lick the salt. The men planned to camp there several weeks. They would boil the water in big kettles until there was only salt left. Then they would take the salt back to the people at Boonesborough.

One day Boone went out hunting alone. Suddenly he was surprised by Indians. They were a war party led by Chief Blackfish. They were on their way to Boonesborough. These Shawnee Indians came from north of Kentucky. They felt that Henderson had no right to claim their hunting grounds. Certainly *they* had not sold Kentucky to him. They might not have been so warlike if the American Revolution had not started. The British were making friends with the Indians everywhere and helping them fight the settlers.

Boone knew how the Shawnees felt about having to share their hunting ground with the white men. But he knew also that he must find a way to save the fort.

"Don't go to Boonesborough now," he told the Indians. "You don't have a big enough war party. Boonesborough is far too strong for you to capture."

This was not true at all. There were not many men at the fort. But Daniel hoped to stall off the Shawnees until Boonesborough had time to send for help.

"Wait until spring," he went on. "Then you won't have to fight. The people will come willingly. I will bring them north to you. Right now it is too cold for the women and the children to travel. But in the spring they will come with you."

Chief Blackfish was delighted to find that Boone was so friendly. He had admired Boone for a long time. He did not know that Boone was trying hard to fool him.

"What about your men?" Chief Blackfish asked.

Boone thought quickly. He knew the Indians had seen the men at the salt licks.

"I will lead you to my men," he told Chief Blackfish, "if you will promise not to kill them."

Chief Blackfish promised. Boone took the Indians to his men.

"We are in great danger," he whispered to them. "We must go north with the Indians, or they will kill us. The fort is in danger too. But perhaps we can escape and warn our families."

At the end of the long journey the Indians and their prisoners reached the Shawnee towns in the north. There, Chief Blackfish told Boone that he wanted him for a son. He made Boone go through a long adoption ceremony and gave him the name of Big Turtle.

Boone liked Chief Blackfish, but he did not really want to be a Shawnee. He pretended to be pleased about becoming the Chief's son, but he only pretended.

One day the Indians went hunting. While they were gone, Boone ran away and started for Boonesborough.

The Indians followed him, but he was too clever for them. They lost his trail. In four days he traveled one hundred and sixty miles.

Finally he reached Boonesborough.

"The Indians are on the way! Get ready to fight!" he told the people.

Soon Chief Blackfish came with over four hundred Shawnees. He called Boone to come outside the fort. Daniel Boone went out bravely.

"Why did you run away?" Chief Blackfish asked Boone.

"I wanted to see my wife and my children," Boone answered.

"You have seen them," the Chief replied. "Now come back with me. You and all your people."

"Give me a little time to think it over," Boone said.

He hoped that help would come from other forts. He waited and waited, but no help came.

"We shall defend the fort as long as a man is living," Boone told the people.

The fight began. The Indians fired at the fort. The white men fired back. Everyone worked hard. The women and the children loaded guns and carried food to the men. The white men were outnumbered, but the Indians did not know this.

The men did not stop fighting for eight days and eight nights. By then everyone was very tired. The Indians had shot flaming torches, and the roofs of the cabins were on fire. Not a drop of water was left in the fort.

"Look! Look!" someone shouted.

The sky had been dark all day. Now it was starting to rain. It rained and it poured. The rain came down and put out the fires. It filled the tubs and pails with water to drink. Everyone felt hopeful again.

When morning came, no Indians were in sight. Every single one of them was gone. They had disappeared into the forest. The fort was saved.

DANIEL BOONE'S REWARD

The Indian raids kept on all over Kentucky. When the American Revolution ended, the British stopped helping the Indians fight the settlers. Some tribes kept on fighting on their own, but finally the settlers defeated the Indians and forced them to sign a treaty. Things slowly became more peaceful.

More and more settlers came west. They came over the Wilderness Road that Boone and his men had made. They came down the Ohio River in big flatboats. These settlers killed game in the forest. They cleared land, grew crops, built houses, and started towns.

Daniel Boone was fifty years old now. One day he discovered that he did not own any of the land he had thought was his.

"This does not seem right," he said. "I was one of the first to come to Kentucky. My life was hard. I risked it for the people many times."

It was not right, but it was true. Boone had been too busy hunting and trapping to put his claims on paper.

Boone lost almost all his land. He tried to farm, but he was not a good farmer. He tried to keep a store, but his heart was not in it. His good wife, Rebecca, often took his place in the store, while Daniel worked as a guide showing new settlers the way down the Ohio River. And he held some jobs with the new government.

One day hunters told Daniel Boone about land farther west near the great Mississippi River. "It's wild and free," they said. "There are bear and deer. There are herds of buffalo. It's the kind of land Kentucky used to be."

"That's the place for me," Boone said. "It's too crowded here. The other day I looked out of the window and saw the smoke of another man's cabin. I'll go west. I want elbow room."

And besides elbow room, he wanted land. He had always dreamed about owning a lot of land.

He was disappointed about losing his claims in Kentucky.

So Boone and his family went west. The land where they settled belonged to Spain. Later it was traded to the French and then bought by America. It is the land we now call Missouri.

The Spaniards were proud to have Daniel Boone live among them. They gave him all the land he wanted. He hunted and trapped in the new country as he had in the old. He sold the furs and skins for a good price.

Then Boone made a trip back to Kentucky. He called together all the people he had once known.

"I owed money to you when I left here," he said. "I want to pay my debts."

When he returned to his family in Missouri, Boone was a poor man again. But he had a smile on his face.

"I am a free man," he said. "I owe nothing to any man. That makes it worth being poor again."

The United States Congress voted to give Boone one thousand acres of land. It was a reward for all he had done in exploring and settling the West. He hunted and fished until he was very old. He never stopped exploring. He was still looking for adventure and elbow room!

But Daniel Boone, traveler, hunter, woodsman, and fighter, will be remembered longest as the man who opened the way to Kentucky.

"Get out of Kentucky and stay out!" the Indians told Daniel Boone. But Daniel Boone did not scare easily.

There was the time his daughter was kidnaped by the Indians. Boone tracked the kidnapers through the forest and rescued her.

There was the time Boone was captured by the Shawnees. He escaped in time to warn the people of Boonesborough: "The Indians are coming! Get ready to fight!"

Boone's life was full of adventure. And this book tells his story.

THE END

Printed in Dunstable, United Kingdom

65274978R00020